ROSÉ MADE
ME DO IT

ROSÉ MADE ME DO IT

60 PERFECTLY PINK PUNCHES AND COCKTAILS

COLLEEN GRAHAM
ILLUSTRATED BY RUBY TAYLOR

HarperCollins*Publishers*

HarperCollins*Publishers*
1 London Bridge Street
London SE1 9GF
www.harpercollins.co.uk

First published by HarperCollins*Publishers* in 2019

10 9 8 7 6 5 4 3 2 1

Copyright © HarperCollins*Publishers*
Written by Colleen Graham
Illustrated by Ruby Taylor
Design by JC Lanaway

Colleen Graham asserts her moral rights as the author of this work.

A catalogue record for this book is available from the British Library

ISBN 978-0-00-834029-2

Printed and bound in Latvia

MIX
Paper from
responsible sources
FSC™ C007454

CONTENTS

INTRODUCTION

Rosé isn't a wine that fits conveniently into one category in terms of style, grape or flavour profile – it's a complex group that includes sweet, dry, still and sparkling wines produced all over the world!

There are, however, three things that rosés do have in common: they're pink (although they vary from pale to surprisingly dark), they pair well with food, and they're fabulous cocktail mixers, the latter being the focus of this book. I won't boggle your mind with the ins and outs of rosé (although you will learn a bit about how it's made and what to expect from certain regions or grape varietals) – there are plenty of books out there that cover all of the finer details. Instead, I want to invite you on the journey of discovering rosé cocktails! Rosé is one of the best wines for mixed drinks, with its flavour of strawberries or watermelon. It works perfectly with many spirits (whisky, gin, vodka, tequila, rum) and almost any additional flavours, from fruits to herbs and spices. And although seen as a summer wine, it's a great fit for cocktails at any time of year.

My goal is to give you some basics on mixing up great cocktails, and to inspire you to explore some unusual flavours. This book includes some incredibly simple drinks – like the Pink Wine Spritzer (see page 32) – as well as a rosé twist on familiar drinks like the mojito and the gin and tonic. There are some very special cocktails that display unique flavour combinations, such as the Lychee Ginger Martini (see page 106) and the Rosemary & Basil Fizz (see page 118). And you'll find that I love to use homemade ingredients. Of course, given the topic, there are also plenty of frosé and sangria recipes. I've found inspiration in the drinks that others have created, and hope to inspire you to take these to a new level. I'm not a wine critic or expert, but a writer who has spent over a decade studying mixed drinks and is grateful to be able to share that knowledge with others. Cocktails are meant to be fun, and wine should be fun. When the two come together, you know a party's on its way!

WHAT IS ROSÉ?

In nature, there are red grapes and white grapes, and within those, hundreds of varietals are used to make red and white wine, respectively. There are, however, no pink grapes, so how does one get the pink wines designated as rosés?

Rosé is not defined by the grape, but by the method. The catch is that since rosés are not varietal-dependent like other styles of wine, they offer a vast range of different flavour profiles. There are sweet rosés, a surprising number of dry rosés and plenty of sparkling rosés to choose from. Rosés are made in every corner of the globe, although there are areas in major wine-making countries that specialise in it. You will notice regional differences at times, just like with other wines, and you will encounter bottles that are a complete gamble. Will it be sweet or dry? Sometimes it's very hard to tell, but that's part of the fun!

If your experience with rosé has been limited to white zinfandel (yes, the sweet wine that captures the attention of many young drinkers is a rosé), then you'll be delighted to know that there really is a rosé for every wine drinker.

HOW IS ROSÉ MADE?

There are a few different methods for making rosé. The most common method used today begins with the juice of red grapes remaining in contact with the grape skin for a few days before the skin is removed. This short period of maceration results in a blush-coloured wine.

A few rosés use a direct pressing method whereby the grapes are pressed with the skins, which are then removed straight away, leaving behind a light pink juice.

A third approach is the *saignée* process (pronounced sehn-yay, French for 'to bleed'). In this case, a little of the red wine juice is 'bled off' early in the maceration process while the wine is still pink. The result is both a useable rosé and a red wine.

Used less often, a fourth technique involves blending a red and white wine together. Some wine-making regions frown upon the method, and many don't regulate it, but a number of rosé Champagnes rely on it.

STYLES OF ROSÉ

Rosé is French for 'pink'; Spanish and Portuguese wines are labelled 'rosado', and Italian wines 'rosato'. However, rosé is definitely not limited to these countries. Understanding the complex maze that is rosé's many flavour characteristics is complicated, so we'll only touch on this briefly to make navigating wine labels a little easier.

Rosé comes in many shades of pink. On the lightest side, you'll find the drier rosés of Provence. This French region primarily makes rosé, offering zesty, refreshing wines that have long been held up as the standard. Following these are the pinot noir rosés, which are slightly earthier, with a bright, acidic fruitiness. Spain's favourite grape – the tempranillo – produces a slightly darker rosé with a brilliant spiced-berry flavour and a slightly darker hue. Surprisingly, when it comes to the rosé colour spectrum, California's famed white zinfandel falls right in the middle. If you're looking for a sweet wine, a bottle of white zin is what you want.

As you move through the remaining red wine grapes, the rosés produced by them tend to get darker. From merlot and sangiovese to cabernet sauvignon and shiraz (or syrah), the pink begins to resemble red wine. The darkest rosés come from Tavel, a small area in France's Rhone Valley that produces nothing but rosé. These offer the best choice for red wine lovers, with the perfect display of tannins against spicy berry flavours and an unusually dry palate.

All of the other styles of rosé produced throughout the world fall somewhere within that spectrum. There are great options from Germany (roséwein or Weissherbst), France's Loire Valley (rosé d'Anjou) and the Austrian state of Styria. The Spanish rosados (including sparkling cavas) are light and fresh, while Portugal tends to produce rosados that are sweet and inexpensive, with a hint of sparkle. Moscato wines are sweeter, and Italy's prosecco rosatos are known for their vivacious bubbles. Beyond all that, there are many rosés that don't fit into any easily defined idea of regional or varietal characteristics.

Before we finish, there are just a few more simple notes to bear in mind. The driest rosés often come from the driest red wine grapes, such as grenache, cinsault and shiraz. Any rosé can be a blend of grapes or use a single varietal, so don't rely on that. A sparkling wine with a label saying 'frizzante' is gently sparkling, and 'brut' means 'dry'. When in doubt, simply read the winemaker's notes on the label. And, if you're intrigued by a bottle (even just the catchy label), try it! If you don't like it on its own, there's bound to be a cocktail that will doctor it up.

DRINKING ROSÉ

Despite all the variations, rosé always has a generalised flavour profile of strawberries or watermelon. It contains fewer tannins than red wines and is very easy to drink. Rosés are typically best when young, too, so drink them up, don't store them!

For the most part, you'll want to chill still rosé before drinking it, and sparkling rosés are best when ice-cold. You are free to stick to your own preferences, but since we're mixing up cold rosé cocktails here, keeping bottles cold will definitely help the drinks along.

You will also be delighted to hear that rosé is the most versatile wine for food pairings. Don't stress over which wine is best with steak or seafood – rosé can cover the entire gamut of foods, cuisines and courses, from canapés to dessert. Likewise, the cocktails you make with rosé will be a splendid match for any meal.

TIPS FOR PERFECT COCKTAILS

Here's the secret to mixing up a great cocktail: have fun!
There are lots of tricks that bartenders use to create spectacular drinks, but anyone can learn the basic techniques (they're not difficult), so the most important thing is to have a good time. You might make mistakes – we all do – and that's okay. It's just a drink that will be gone in a few minutes; the real joy in mixing cocktails is the exploration, discovering what you like and don't like.

That said, a few tips will help you make the best cocktails possible:

• Use premium-quality spirits that you wouldn't mind drinking on their own. There's no need to pay for a super pricey bottle of rosé, though, as wine is typically a cocktail mixer that allows you to save a bit of money.

• Fresh ingredients are best. This is particularly true of citrus juices, but if you have the ability to juice other fruits, say with an electric juicer, that's even better. And don't be afraid of homemade mixers like Simple Syrup (see page 15) – they're easy, cheap and fun.

• Chill your glassware, especially if the cocktail recipe doesn't include ice in the glass. Your drinks will stay colder longer and be more refreshing.

If you find a drink that you think needs to be tweaked, by all means do it! Cocktail recipes are meant to be adjusted according to personal taste, and everyone's tastes are different. After all, I'm not drinking it – you are.

BAR GEAR

There's no need to buy a full bar kit unless you'd like to. With just a few of the essentials, you can mix up a great variety of drinks.

A cocktail shaker is a must. A standard three-piece shaker with a built-in strainer will do most home bartenders just fine. Stainless steel shakers are the best and will last a lifetime. If you go the pro route and pick up a Boston shaker (one piece is a shaking tin and the other a mixing glass), be sure to buy a Hawthorne strainer as well.

A bar spoon is also a good investment because the long, twisted handle makes stirring a breeze, especially in tall glasses. For precise measuring, a jigger (a two-ended cup that measures shots and half-shots) is invaluable and allows for the greatest control of flavour balance. Finally, add a muddler to your shopping list. The freshest cocktails – mojitos and juleps included – require this handy stick, resembling a miniature baseball bat. (More on this on page 12.)

ICE

It's a given that high-quality ingredients will produce better-tasting mixed drinks, and the same rule applies to ice. It is the one ingredient that almost every cocktail has in common, so it's extremely important!

You will use a lot of ice, both in the serving glass and/or the cocktail shaker. Make your ice with distilled water for the best results, and do always have a fresh stock of ice in the freezer so that you don't run out. If there's a tray that's been sitting there for a couple of months unused, toss it away and start again. Try to avoid storing ice near fish and other pungent frozen foods, too, because it will absorb some of their flavours. Fishy drinks are definitely not good!

For a drink like the Berry Rosé Julep (see page 30), you'll need shaved ice (okay, it's not necessary, but it is really nice). If you don't have an ice maker that has that capability, toss some ice in your blender and give it a few whirls, then get rid of any excess water. Another fun way to crush ice (a little chunkier than shaved ice) is to whack it with your muddler. Put some ice cubes in a sealable plastic bag or a Lewis bag (made of cloth just for this purpose) and whack it into smaller bits. It's also an activity that provides great stress relief!

A couple of the recipes also utilise novelty ice cubes as part of the drink. The Rosé Parade (see page 92) freezes wine into ice cubes, while the Sparkling Borage Cocktail (see page 70) and the Blushing Fizz (see page 96) both freeze flowers inside the ice.

SHAKING AND STIRRING

There are two primary methods for mixing cocktails: shaking and stirring. They're both easy, but there are tricks to doing it right. For the first, fill the cocktail shaker with ice (about five or six cubes). Shake for at least 10 seconds or until the outside of the shaker gets nice and frosty. Some drinks are stirred and you'll want to do this with a smooth, steady turn of the wrist (keep your elbow still, it's not cake batter!) for at least 30 seconds.

With either technique, always strain out the mixing ice unless the recipe indicates otherwise. The agitation during mixing breaks down the ice so it will melt faster, resulting in a drink that quickly becomes watered down. For drinks served on the rocks, use fresh ice in the serving glass.

MUDDLING

The fresher the drinks you want to mix up, the more you will fall in love with muddling. It's a fantastic mixing technique used to juice the majority of fruits and to extract the essence from herbs, creating a flavoursome crushed base for a drink out of fresh ingredients. Once you learn the value of a muddler, you'll wonder where this amazing tool has been all your life!

The process of muddling is incredibly simple: place the ingredients to be muddled in the bottom of a mixing glass or shaker and press them with the flat end of the muddler until well mixed (a minute or two usually does it). Use a twisting motion with your wrist as you push down to accentuate the mixing.

Fruits that are to be muddled should be cut into small pieces (a few centimetres). Citrus fruits work well as half slices and wedges, and there is no need to remove the peel. For leafy herbs like mint and basil, tear the leaves or slap them between your palms before dropping them into the glass to maximise the flavour. Other herbs (such as lavender and rosemary) and spices can be tossed in whole, as long as any stems have been removed beforehand.

SPARKLING ROSÉ
Quite a few of the recipes you'll find in this book call for sparkling rosé. If you already have a bottle of still rosé open, don't rush to the shops for a bottle of bubbly; you can mimic sparkling rosé by adding a little soda water to still rosé. Just a couple of splashes in a glass or so of wine will give a nice effervescence without overly diluting it. The other option is to add a splash of soda water directly to the drink after pouring the still wine.

SANGRIAS AND PUNCHES
We're dealing with wine recipes here, so you should expect to find a few sangrias and other wine punches. Each recipe was written for 170ml (6fl oz) servings, and the number of servings each recipe produces is indicated. If you need more or less punch, simply increase or decrease each ingredient accordingly, as long as you always keep the ingredients in proportion.

You'll also see that the sangria recipes suggest 'marrying' the flavours by chilling the drink overnight. This is the best way to create punches that use fresh fruits. As they sit, the liquids absorb the taste of the fruits, giving you a concoction the following day that is one beautiful blend of flavours!

IN THE BLENDER

Yes, even rosé can end up in a frozen cocktail! If you haven't enjoyed a frosé yet, you're in for a real treat. For the best blended drinks, chop the ice and any fruits in the blender before adding the liquid ingredients.

Most recipes call for around a cup of ice, which is five or six average-sized cubes. After blending, if the result is a little too thin for your taste, add one or two more ice cubes and blend again. And if the cocktail is too thick? Add a splash of one of the drink's liquid ingredients.

DRESS IT UP

Garnishes are often an afterthought, especially if you're just mixing up a drink for yourself. But they do look pretty, and they can help to make a good impression when serving guests, so it's a good idea to practise creating them as often as you can. Additions such as citrus slices and twists, as well as herbs, can add to the flavour of a drink, too. You can squeeze a little juice in as you drink, gently press a lemon twist over the cocktail to express its essence, or drop in something like rosemary and let the herb's flavour slowly infuse into the liquid. The smallest touches often take a cocktail from okay to spectacular.

Rimming a glass is another fun option that can be used with almost any cocktail. In these pages, for example, you'll find the No Way Rosé Margarita (see page 54), which calls for a sugar rim. Begin by wetting the rim of the glass with a liquid in the recipe (with many cocktails, a citrus wedge works perfectly). Then roll the rim of the glass around in a small dish filled with white granulated sugar until it's coated evenly. Still holding the glass upside down, gently tap off any excess sugar and you're ready to pour the drink. This fancy little trick goes a step further with the Birthday Cake Mimosa (see page 94), in which you'll dip the rim first into some delicious icing, followed by some coloured sprinkles!

SYRUPS

As much as I love to muddle, my fascination with Simple Syrup is even greater. It is the one ingredient in the bar that you have absolute control over, and it's the perfect sweetener for cold drinks because the sugar's already been dissolved before it is added to the drink.

Many of the recipes in this book rely on homemade syrups with bespoke flavour infusions that you'll be hard pressed to find in the shops. All of these are made using Simple Syrup, and details of these are given on pages 16–17. And plain Simple Syrup itself is used even more often; once you learn its dirty little secret, you'll never waste your money buying it again!

What is Simple Syrup? Water and sugar! It's really that simple. In a pinch, you can even combine the two ingredients in your cocktail shaker, shake it up, and *voilà*. That's called 'bar syrup', and it will do, but there is a standard Simple Syrup recipe that you'll turn to time and again on your cocktail adventures:

In a small saucepan, bring 250ml (8½fl oz) of water to the boil. Add 225g (8oz) of sugar and stir constantly until it has dissolved completely. Cover the pan, reduce the heat and then simmer for 15 minutes. Let the syrup cool before bottling it in a tightly sealed jar. This will produce 250ml (8½fl oz) of syrup, which will keep well in the refrigerator for a week or two.

Now that you know the secrets to Simple Syrup, it's time to add flavour! The possibilities are endless, and you can make single-ingredient syrups or create custom blends with complementary flavours. These homemade syrups provide a great way to get the taste of fresh ingredients into an easy-to-mix sweetener.

The additional ingredients you'll need to add to the basic syrup recipe in order to create each of the homemade syrups mentioned in this book are provided opposite. The individual recipes will then guide you through the process of making them.

For all syrups, the general technique is to add the flavouring ingredient (chopped fruit or whole herbs and spices) after turning the syrup down to a simmer, then let it steep in the syrup until it has cooled down completely. Before bottling, strain out any solid pieces so that you are left with a clean flavoured syrup.

Use the syrup for the intended cocktail, then explore its potential in other drinks – any syrup can be topped with soda water for a homemade soft drink, many will work as a sweetener for lemonade or iced tea, and some are perfect for hot drinks like coffee and tea (especially the cinnamon syrup).

Three recipes call for honey syrup, which enables you to add the flavour of honey to a drink in a form that is easier to mix. Honey syrup is made with equal parts of honey and water, stirred until they reach a uniform consistency. You can make just enough for each cocktail.

FLAVOURED SYRUPS USED IN THE RECIPES

Lavender syrup: used in the Lavender Pink Lemonade (page 42); add 3 tablespoons of lavender flowers.

Rose syrup: used in the No Way Rosé Margarita (page 54); add 120ml (4fl oz) of rose water.

Strawberry syrup: optional in The Frosé (page 56); add 3 large strawberries and ¼ teaspoon of vanilla extract (optional, but recommended).

Basil syrup: used in the Watermelon Frosé (page 64); add 20g (¾oz) of basil leaves.

Borage syrup: used in the Sparkling Borage Cocktail (page 70); add a handful of borage flowers and young leaves.

Rosemary syrup: used in the Rosaquiri (page 76); add 1 or 2 sprigs of rosemary.

Thyme syrup: used in the Rosé Sour (page 78); add 5 large sprigs of thyme.

Vanilla-lavender syrup: used in the Blushing Fizz (page 96); add 7g (¼oz) of lavender buds and 1 vanilla pod.

Sage-lime syrup: used in the Sage Gimlet (page 100); add a few sage leaves and the juice of 1 lime.

Lychee syrup: used in the Lychee Ginger Martini (page 106); add 85g (3oz) of hulled fresh lychees.

Rosemary-basil syrup: used in the Rosemary & Basil Fizz (page 118); add 1 sprig of rosemary and 20g (¾oz) of basil leaves.

Cinnamon syrup: used in the Poinsettia Sangria (page 122); add 1 cinnamon stick.

Plain honey syrup: is found in the Sweet Honey Rosé (page 104) and the Rosé Collins (page 114) recipes. The Tea for You & Me recipe (page 84) adds the juice of a lime to honey syrup.

INFUSIONS

Another fun way to add a twist of flavour to cocktails is with the use of infusions. Infusions are created using a spirit – most often vodka or rum, although other spirits are not off-limits. Some of the flavours you'll find in the recipes can be found commercially, but others will not be available, so you will need to create these at home.

Homemade infusions are even easier to make than flavoured syrups, though most take far longer. You'll need to plan ahead – anywhere from a day to several weeks – to allow the flavours to develop fully; when that is will be a matter of personal taste, but guidelines are given in each case. The only tools you'll require are infusion jars (wide-mouthed with a tight seal and large enough to hold the desired amount of alcohol), a straining system (a fine mesh strainer and/or some muslin), and a knife to cut up any ingredients. Beyond that, all you'll need is patience.

Fruits need to be rinsed and cut up; spices can be left whole, and entire sprigs of herbs can be used once rinsed. Place the ingredient in a jar, fill it with the alcohol, shake, then leave it in a cool, dark place. Shake the jar once a day to wake everything up. Taste the infusion towards the end of the time and let it rest longer if needed. Once the flavour reaches your desired intensity, strain out the solid ingredients and bottle your new spirit – no refrigeration is needed.

Generally, the quantity of flavouring ingredient is not dependent on the amount of alcohol – two teabags will infuse a bottle of rum just as well as they will flavour 90ml (3fl oz) of rum for a single drink. The volume difference may simply require a longer or shorter infusion time. However, it is worth making at least half a bottle at a time, since you can then use the infusion in other cocktails. The homemade infusions that you'll need for some of the recipes in this book are shown opposite. As with the syrups, full instructions are then provided within the relevant recipes.

INFUSIONS USED IN THE RECIPES

Chilli-infused citrus vodka: used in the Spicy Spritzer (page 36); starting with a citrus vodka (buy it or make your own), you'll need 2 whole chillies and an infusion of just 2 hours (it gets hot very fast).

Citrus-infused vodka: (extremely easy to find commercially): potentially used for the chilli-infused citrus vodka above, but needs to be done separately and first because citrus fruits require a much longer infusion. Use a combination of lemons, limes and oranges (1 of each fruit for an entire bottle works well) to create a custom blend. Rinse the fruit and cut into slices. Infuse for 3 days to a full week.

Pomegranate-infused vodka: (very easy to find commercially): used in the Pomegranate Grapefruit Frosé (page 62); requires 1 pomegranate crushed in vodka, and infused for 5 days.

Tea-infused rum: used in the Tea for You & Me (page 84); requires 2 teabags and a 1-day infusion.

Grapefruit-infused tequila: used in the Rosé Sunrise (page 102); requires 1 whole grapefruit, cut into slices, and an infusion of 3 to 5 days.

Ginger-infused vodka: (very limited commercial availability): used in the Lychee Ginger Martini (page 106); requires 50g (1¾oz) of sliced ginger and about 7 days for the infusion.

Cucumber-infused vodka: (limited commercial availability): used in the Rosemary & Basil Fizz (page 118); requires 1 cucumber and potentially 2 weeks of infusing.

Mango-infused rum: (commercially available): used in the White Peach Sangria (page 126); requires 1 mango and at least a week for the infusion.

THE RECIPES

ROSÉ 75

One of the best-known Champagne cocktails around, the French 75 has been a favourite celebratory drink since it was created sometime around World War I. As you can imagine, it has taken a number of turns over the last century. In fact, it's rare to find two identical French 75 recipes. So let's keep changing it up, skip the Champagne, and pour a sparkling rosé instead! Rosé is a lovely wine for this simple drink, and the pink bubbles give it a new life in the glass. While the majority of drinkers today prefer gin in a French 75, brandy (specifically Cognac) has been an option for years and it's actually a slightly better fit for rosé. This is especially true if you have a drier wine – the brandy will add a delectable hint of sweetness that gin simply can't provide.

Ingredients
45ml (1½fl oz) brandy
8ml (¼fl oz) Simple Syrup (see page 15)
15ml (½fl oz) fresh lemon juice
sparkling rosé, to top up
a lemon twist, to garnish

Instructions
In a cocktail shaker filled with ice, combine the brandy, Simple Syrup and juice. Shake well and strain into a flute. Top up with sparkling rosé and decorate with a lemon twist.

ROSÉ & TONIC

The Rosé & Tonic is a little dry and a little sweet, which makes it a fabulous dinner drink. Pair it with seafood, or any meat or vegetarian dish that features plenty of savoury herbs and spices, and you're in for a real treat. Tonic water has a dry profile and is a natural palate cleanser, so it's always an excellent companion to a meal. Rosé is also a very versatile wine for food pairings, and it contributes a touch of sweetness. The lime brings it all together, adding a hint of tartness both in the drink and on your lips. It's a delightful balance that can make almost any meal more enjoyable.

Ingredients
90ml (3fl oz) rosé
90ml (3fl oz) tonic water
a lime wedge

Instructions
Pour the wine into a tall glass filled with ice, then add the tonic water. Rub the lime wedge around the rim of the glass, then squeeze the juice into the drink and drop the wedge into the glass.

ROSÉ MOJITO

(serves 6–8)

Mojitos are a ton of fun to drink and not as hard to make as you might think. The secret is to use a muddler to press the fresh mint into the syrup. This flavour foundation can then be dressed up in the original way (rum and soda water) or it can take a more unconventional turn, as with the Rosé Mojito. 'Refreshing' doesn't even begin to describe the taste; you'll love how the cooling, sweetened mint plays off a nice rosé. It is then given an extra twist by using a sparkling lemonade rather than soda water. If you prefer it less sweet, add a lemon-flavoured Italian soda water instead.

Ingredients
2 limes, cut into wedges
25g (1oz) fresh mint leaves
Simple Syrup (see page 15), to taste
750ml (25fl oz) rosé
480ml (16fl oz) sparkling lemonade
lime slices and extra mint leaves, to garnish

Instructions
Using a muddler, press the lime wedges, mint leaves and about 15ml (½fl oz) of Simple Syrup in a jug to release the juice and essential oils. Add the rosé and lemonade. Stir well, taste and add more syrup if desired. The jug can then be stored in the fridge for an hour or two. Serve in tall glasses filled with ice and garnish with lime slices and fresh mint.

Tip: If your mint is beginning to wilt, you can make a mint-infused Simple Syrup ahead of time instead. Use a lot of mint so that the flavour is intense – you then won't have to add more syrup later, which would result in an overly sweet drink.

STRAWBERRY MOJITO

Strawberry season is the perfect time to mix up this delightful mojito for yourself. Sweet, juicy strawberries go perfectly with rum and mint and take the place of the cocktail's traditional limes – and of course there's a rosé twist that you're going to love. You'll find this cocktail to be an excellent place to use your favourite light rum – most will pair perfectly with any rosé you choose. Although you will muddle the strawberries, mint and syrup, it's not a bad idea to use an old bartender's trick to wake up the mint – simply slap the leaves in the palm of your hand before adding them to the glass. It's a quick step that can have quite an impact on the drink's flavour.

Ingredients
3 strawberries, hulled and sliced
a handful of fresh mint
15ml (½fl oz) Simple Syrup (see page 15)
45ml (1½fl oz) light rum
90ml (3fl oz) rosé
soda water, to top up
an extra strawberry, lime and a sprig of mint, to garnish

Instructions
In the bottom of a tall glass, muddle the strawberries, mint and Simple Syrup. Fill the glass with ice and add the rum and wine. Stir well, then top up with a splash of soda water. Garnishing the drink with a single strawberry and a small sprig of mint is a nice finishing touch.

BERRY ROSÉ JULEP

The Berry Rosé Julep puts a berrylicious twist on the classic mint julep. It's perfect for warm weather affairs, whether you're enjoying some time with friends or just want to slip out onto the patio for a relaxing afternoon in the sun on your own. Choose a nice, smooth whisky for this drink – something like a softer bourbon or an Irish blended whiskey is ideal against the fresh berries. This drink also substitutes rosemary for the traditional mint, creating a sweet floral touch that is quite lovely against the pink wine. Add more berries if you like, and mix raspberries with blackberries if you have both on hand.

Ingredients
5–6 raspberries and/or blackberries
a sprig of rosemary
45ml (1 ½fl oz) whisky
rosé, to top up
extra rosemary and berries, to garnish

Instructions
In the bottom of a tumbler, muddle the berries and rosemary. Add the whisky, then fill the glass with shaved ice. Top up with rosé, garnish with rosemary and a few berries, and enjoy it through a straw.

PINK WINE SPRITZER

Sometimes you will open a bottle of rosé only to find that it's not quite what you expected. That doesn't necessarily mean it's bad – it may simply need a little help. In these moments, turn to the Pink Wine Spritzer, a simple recipe that can give any rosé a boost. There are no fancy tricks here, just a little sparkling soda water added to a still rosé. The key is to make sure that both ingredients are well chilled before mixing them. Not only is this a great drink on its own, and fabulously easy to mix up, you will also find it useful if you want to create a cocktail that calls for sparkling rosé, but you don't happen to have a bottle of the bubbly version available. In fact, soda water added to any still wine will allow you to enjoy the same sparkling effect for very little cost.

Ingredients
90ml (3fl oz) chilled rosé
30ml (1fl oz) chilled soda water

Instructions
Pour the rosé into a white-wine glass, then top it off with the ice-cold soda water.

ROSÉ APEROL SPRITZ

The Rosé Aperol Spritz is a great drink to accompany a meal. It pairs well with a variety of foods, from seafood to red meat, and is fabulous with multi-course dinners that involve a wide variety of flavours. It's a refreshing and easy cocktail worthy of any dinner party. Aperol is an orange-coloured aperitif with a bitter orange flavour that will wake up your taste buds and get them ready for the delicious food that you've prepared. While this drink is often made with a sparkling white wine, it's extra special when prepared with a sparkling rosé. The soda water is there to give the bubbles a boost.

Ingredients
60ml (2fl oz) Aperol
90ml (3fl oz) sparkling rosé
a splash of soda water
an orange slice, to garnish

Instructions
Fill a white-wine glass with ice, then add the Aperol and sparkling rosé. Top with a splash of soda water and decorate the glass with the orange slice.

SPICY SPRITZER

Rosé is not out of the question when you're in the mood for a spicy cocktail. You simply have to treat the two flavours in a delicate manner and keep things simple. That's exactly what you'll find in the Spicy Spritzer, a funky twist on the Pink Wine Spritzer (see page 32). The spice in this cocktail comes from a quick infusion of chilli in a citrus vodka. You can use any type of chilli, although Thai chillies and jalapeños are excellent choices. Then, to balance the drink, use soda water if you have a sweeter rosé, or ginger ale if the wine is on the drier side.

Ingredients
2 chillies
45ml (1½fl oz) citrus vodka (see page 19)
90ml (3fl oz) rosé
a splash of soda water or ginger ale
an orange slice, to garnish

Instructions
Simply place a couple of chillies in the amount of vodka you'd like to infuse, then taste it after 2 hours. Leave it to infuse a little longer if you'd like it even spicier. This is a fast infusion, so keep testing it and remove the chillies as soon as it reaches your desired intensity. Pour the infused vodka and wine into a tumbler filled with ice. Top with a splash of soda water or ginger ale, stir, and add an orange slice.

GLAMOUR GIRL MARTINI

Mix up the girliest of all pink martinis and enjoy a very fruity cocktail. This is definitely one to make for special occasions, and it's a fabulous choice for hen nights, birthday parties and anniversaries. With the Glamour Girl Martini, you'll enjoy the fruity combination of peach and cranberry backed by pink wine. It's a lovely drink and, as an added bonus, the wine base makes it lighter on the alcohol than most regular martinis, so one drink won't leave you tipsy.

Ingredients
90ml (3fl oz) rosé
30ml (1fl oz) peach schnapps
15ml (½fl oz) cranberry juice
a cherry, to garnish

Instructions
Pour all three ingredients into a cocktail shaker filled with ice. Shake well, strain into a chilled martini glass and top with a cherry.

ROSÉ COSMO

The classic cosmopolitan is an ideal cocktail for a little rosé. It already has the sweet fruits that pair so nicely with rosé, and the recipe is not too different from the original, so it's both familiar and novel. For the Rosé Cosmo, the wine and citrus vodka play equal roles to form a pretty foundation. This then gets a slight accent from triple sec and cranberry juice to produce a well-balanced cocktail that's easy to drink. In true cosmopolitan fashion, add as much cranberry juice as you like; this recipe produces a drier cosmo that can easily be sweetened by doubling or tripling the juice.

Ingredients

45ml (1½fl oz) citrus vodka
45ml (1½fl oz) rosé
15ml (½fl oz) triple sec
15ml (½fl oz) cranberry juice
an orange twist, to garnish

Instructions

Combine the ingredients in a cocktail shaker filled with ice and shake well. Strain into a chilled martini glass and decorate the rim with an orange twist.

LAVENDER PINK LEMONADE

On a hot summer day, nothing is quite as refreshing as a tall glass of lemonade. It's incredibly easy to make lemonade from scratch – all you need is sugar, lemon juice and water. A glass of Lavender Pink Lemonade gives that formula a funky, fresh twist. This recipe begins with a lavender-infused syrup and is best made with freshly squeezed lemon juice. The water of traditional lemonade is then replaced with a good dose of rosé, which turns this popular drink into a stunning wine cocktail for an afternoon in the garden. Though the recipe makes just a single glass, it's easy to mix up for a party. Simply keep the syrup and juice equal at one part each, then use three parts wine. Pour it all into a jug with ice and stir well. Be sure to sample it and adjust the sweet and sour ingredients to suit your taste.

Ingredients
30ml (1fl oz) lavender syrup
30ml (1fl oz) fresh lemon juice
90ml (3fl oz) rosé
a lemon wedge, to garnish

Instructions
Make the lavender syrup in advance by infusing the Simple Syrup recipe on page 15 with 3 tablespoons of lavender flowers. Pour the lavender syrup, lemon juice and rosé into a cocktail shaker filled with ice and shake well. Strain the drink into a highball glass filled with fresh ice and complete it with a lemon wedge.

WATERMELON CUCUMBER COOLER

Watermelon and cucumber go together like strawberries and cream. This garden-fresh duo is used to make some amazing cocktails, and the Watermelon Cucumber Cooler is one of them. The gin you choose to pour into this drink will make a big difference. While juniper-forward options like a traditional London dry gin make a good drink, it's even better with a gin that has a softer profile. Two favourites are Hendrick's and Aviation American Gin; the former features rose petals and cucumber, while the latter has a floral bouquet dominated by lavender. There are other gins that would work wonderfully, too – just keep in mind that you want to accent (not contradict) the sweet and cooling fruits.

Ingredients
2 cucumber slices
3 watermelon cubes
15ml (½fl oz) Simple Syrup (see page 15)
45ml (1½fl oz) gin
15ml (½fl oz) lime juice
90ml (3fl oz) sparkling rosé
an extra cucumber slice and a watermelon wedge, to garnish

Instructions
In the bottom of a tall glass, muddle the cucumber, watermelon and Simple Syrup thoroughly to release all the fruit juices. Fill the glass with ice, then add the gin, lime juice and sparkling wine, and stir well. Decorate the glass with the extra cucumber and watermelon.

KIR

A staple of French cafés, the Kir has been a popular wine
cocktail for decades because of its fabulous simplicity.
It was popularised by Félix Kir, the mayor of Dijon in
Burgundy after World War II, who frequently served this local
drink to show off two of the area's finest products – wine and
crème de cassis. It remains an impressive cocktail today,
and deserving of the French treatment. When it comes to
creating a balanced drink, the Kir is best with a dry wine
because the blackcurrant liqueur is very sweet. The rosés
produced in France's Provence region are absolutely
perfect because they tend to be among the driest pink
wines produced. While the regular Kir is made with still
wine, you can also make a Kir Royale with a sparkling rosé,
or a Kir Imperial with a still rosé and Chambord. No matter
how you make it, this one's a great choice for dinner.

Ingredients
15ml (½fl oz) crème de cassis
chilled dry rosé, to top up
raspberries, to garnish

Instructions
Pour the crème de cassis into a stemmed wine glass, then top
up with rosé. Garnish with a few raspberries floating in the drink.

ROSÉ BELLINI

A popular choice for brunch, the Bellini is a fabulously simple cocktail. It offers a delightful peach background for sparkling wine and will pair wonderfully with all of your favourite mid-morning foods. In the Rosé Bellini, the customary Champagne is replaced with a sparkling rosé. The drier your wine, the better – the peach nectar imparts enough sweetness to balance out the drink. And this recipe doesn't just swap in the rosé; it is also made a little bit rosier with a splash of rose water, which adds a lovely floral touch – just make sure it's food-grade. While it's highly recommended and accents this peach cocktail perfectly, you can choose to skip it and still enjoy a delightful drink.

Ingredients
60ml (2fl oz) peach nectar, juice or purée
sparkling rosé, to top up
a splash of rose water

Instructions
Pour the peach nectar into a flute. Top up with sparkling rosé, then add a splash of rose water.

PINEAPPLE MIMOSA

Mimosas for everyone! This sparkling orange cocktail is an absolute joy to play around with, as there are so many fruity possibilities to try. One popular rendition is the Pineapple Mimosa, which gives the drink a tropical spin that's perfect for a summertime brunch. This recipe produces a drink that is just a little stronger than the average mimosa because it uses pineapple vodka. The pineapple doesn't stop there, either! To double up on the flavour, you blend pineapple juice with orange juice before adding your chosen sparkling rosé. Have fun with the garnish, too. With the help of a cocktail stick you can make an elaborate 'flag' using a pineapple wedge and a cherry to really dress up the glass.

Ingredients
30ml (1fl oz) pineapple vodka
15ml (½fl oz) triple sec
15ml (½fl oz) orange juice
15ml (½fl oz) pineapple juice
sparkling rosé, to top up
a pineapple wedge and a cherry, to garnish

Instructions
Pour the vodka, triple sec and both juices into a flute.
Top up with sparkling rosé and garnish with a pineapple–cherry skewer.

POMEGRANATE MIMOSA

As festive as it is lovely, the Pomegranate Mimosa will allow you to carry your love for mimosas into the winter. It's the ideal cocktail for a holiday brunch, when you can pick up a fresh pomegranate and harvest the arils (seeds) for a seasonal garnish. The pomegranate flavouring, though, comes from pomegranate liqueur. This is typically ruby red and creates a stunning-looking cocktail. You can also make a fresh grenadine (pomegranate-flavoured syrup) to use instead, and even mix that with a little vodka to create your own rendition of the liqueur. The soda water is added to boost a still rosé, but you can pour a sparkling rosé and skip the soda water if you prefer. If you're feeling particularly merry, a sprig of rosemary makes a fun garnish. This will infuse slowly in the drink and create a subtle but sensational extra layer of flavour.

Ingredients
45ml (1½fl oz) pomegranate liqueur
15ml (½fl oz) triple sec
90ml (3fl oz) rosé
a splash of soda water
pomegranate seeds, rosemary, to garnish

Instructions
Pour the liqueur and triple sec into a flute and add the rosé. Finish the drink with a splash of soda water for sparkle, and decorate the glass with a few pomegranate arils or rosemary.

NO WAY ROSÉ MARGARITA

If it seems like you can add rosé to nearly any cocktail, the answer is that you can! The classic margarita is definitely not off-limits, and it's a lot of fun when you add the flavours of both rosé and rose. The No Way Rosé Margarita is based on the original margarita recipe, which is fantastically refreshing and easier to mix up than most people think. In this variation, we keep the margarita's traditional trio of tequila, lime juice and triple sec, then add a rose-flavoured syrup and a little rosé. It's a simple twist but a lovely one, and an absolute delight to drink.

Ingredients
a splash of rose syrup
white sugar
45ml (1½fl oz) tequila
30ml (1fl oz) fresh lime juice
15ml (½fl oz) triple sec
60ml (2fl oz) rosé
a lime twist, sugar, to garnish

Instructions
Begin by creating the rose syrup by adding 120ml (4fl oz) of rose water to the Simple Syrup recipe on page 15. If desired, moisten the rim of a cocktail or margarita glass and dip it in sugar. In a cocktail shaker filled with ice, combine all the ingredients. Shake well, then strain into the prepared glass and garnish with a lime twist.

THE FROSÉ

It may have started as a trend, but The Frosé is a drink that will be enjoyed for many years to come. And if there is one cocktail that rosé is specifically known for, this is it! It has been instrumental in the pink wine's rise in popularity over the last few years. The Frosé is, essentially, a slushie in which you can blend any variety of fruits. The basic recipe features strawberries, which is the best fruit pairing for rosé. You can add the fruit to some Simple Syrup to make a strawberry-flavoured syrup (see page 17 for quantities), but it's much easier to toss it directly into the blender. And a supply of washed, hulled and sliced strawberries (or any fruit of choice) kept in the freezer will make things even quicker. With any frosé, the wine will lose a bit of colour and flavour, so it's best to choose a darker, fuller-flavoured rosé.

Ingredients
332g (11½oz) strawberries, hulled and sliced
150g (5oz) ice
750ml (25fl oz) rosé
2 tbsp white granulated sugar, or to taste
extra strawberry slices, to garnish

Instructions
Put the strawberries and ice in a blender and blitz lightly. Add the rosé and sugar, then blend until smooth. Pour into tall, chilled glasses and garnish with strawberry slices. If it's not thick enough, add a little more ice – you may need as much as 300g (10oz), depending on your preference – and blend again. Likewise, add more sugar if you'd like it sweeter. You can also store any excess frosé in the freezer until you're ready for another drink.

COCONUT & MANGO FROSÉ

Cool down on a hot summer day with a delicious Coconut & Mango Frosé. It's sweet and inviting, with a tropical flavour that is sure to transport you to some faraway island paradise. The recipe comes with a couple of options for two of the ingredients; choose whichever you prefer or is easiest to find. While coconut rum is very common, if you can find a coconut-flavoured vodka, you might enjoy that a little more. Likewise, if you can't find fresh mangoes at the supermarket, pick up some mango nectar instead.

Ingredients
2 fresh mango slices or 30ml (1fl oz) mango nectar
150g (5oz) ice
30ml (1fl oz) coconut rum or vodka
90ml (3fl oz) rosé
15ml (½fl oz) lemon juice
15ml (½fl oz) Simple Syrup (see page 15)
mango and lemon slices, to garnish

Instructions
Place the mango and ice in a blender and blitz lightly. Add the other ingredients and blend until smooth. Pour into a stemmed tall glass and garnish with slices of mango and lemon.

BLACK FROSÉ

Sometimes you just have to step away from the cute pink drinks and mix one up that's dark and mysterious. While there are no secrets to the Black Frosé, it does have a deep purple colour that is a complete change of pace from most rosé recipes, which is what makes it so much fun. This is probably one of the easiest frosés variants you can make because it requires just four simple ingredients. The fruits are then backed up by a shot of Chambord, although you can substitute any other black raspberry liqueur you like.

Ingredients
100g (3½oz) blackberries
150g (5oz) ice
45ml (1½fl oz) Chambord
90ml (3fl oz) rosé
extra berries, to garnish

Instructions
Place the berries and ice in a blender and give them a quick blitz. Add the Chambord and wine, then blend until smooth. Pour into a tall hurricane glass, or piña colada glass, and garnish with a few berries.

POMEGRANATE GRAPEFRUIT FROSÉ

A beautiful blushing pink, the Pomegranate Grapefruit Frosé is as stunning to look at as it is to drink. This wine slushie deserves some beautiful glassware, so pull out a piece of your fancy stemware to serve it in – a coupe, a large red-wine glass or a margarita glass. The flavour combination of pomegranate and grapefruit is an absolute delight. Pomegranate vodkas are easy to find, but you can also make your own using the fresh fruit when it's in season. It just so happens that the pomegranate and grapefruit seasons coincide in the middle of winter, so this frosé is a wonderful way to forget about the cold for a few minutes!

Ingredients
30ml (1fl oz) pomegranate vodka
150g (5oz) ice
90ml (3fl oz) rosé
30ml (1fl oz) grapefruit juice
a splash of lemon juice
15ml (½fl oz) Simple Syrup (see page 15)
a sprig of fresh mint or thyme, to garnish

Instructions
Blitz the ice in a blender, then add all of the ingredients and blend until smooth. Pour into a large coupe or red-wine glass and garnish with a sprig of mint or thyme.

If you choose to make the pomegranate vodka, add some pomegranate arils (seeds) to a clear vodka in an infusion jar. Crush the arils using a muddler to release their juice, then let it sit for about 5 days before straining and bottling.

WATERMELON FROSÉ

(serves 6)

The beauty of frosés is that you can use all sorts of
ingredients to create them. Quite often, you can take
inspiration from flavour pairings used in foods, such as fruit
salads. That's what happened with this Watermelon Frosé,
and it is certainly not a one-dimensional taste! It turns out
that both watermelon and blueberries are a perfect match
for basil, and all three are really nice against a rosé
background. While the herb itself does not blend well, a
simple syrup that extracts the flavour from its leaves does.
The Watermelon Frosé is perfect for a summer barbecue,
so it's made by the jug. After all, something this delicious is
too good to keep to yourself.

Ingredients

60ml (2fl oz) basil syrup
150g (5oz) watermelon, cubed
100g (3½oz) blueberries
150g (5oz) ice
750ml (25fl oz) rosé
2 tbsp sugar, to taste
watermelon wedges, blueberries and basil leaves, to garnish

Instructions

To make the basil syrup, add 20g (¾oz) of basil leaves to
the Simple Syrup recipe on page 15. Place the watermelon,
berries and ice in a blender and blitz lightly. Add the basil
syrup and the other ingredients and blend until smooth
(adding more ice if you prefer a thicker drink). Pour into tall
glasses (Mason jars are ideal) and garnish each with a small
watermelon wedge, a few blueberries and a basil leaf.

SOMETHING BLUE

When you're tired of mixing all the pink cocktails, switch to Something Blue (literally!). This beautiful and elegant cocktail was designed for weddings and hen parties, but is a perfect fit for any special occasion – or just an afternoon with friends. The star of this show is Hpnotiq, an alluring ocean-blue liqueur that's filled with tropical fruit juices, French vodka and a kiss of Cognac. The taste really does live up to the description, and it is spectacular with a dry rosé. Although this recipe makes a single glass, this is another one that can easily be made by the jug. Keep the quantities of liqueur and wine equal, then add half as much ginger ale just prior to serving to ensure it's delightfully bubbly.

Ingredients
60ml (2fl oz) Hpnotiq
60ml (2fl oz) dry rosé
a splash of lemon juice
30ml (1fl oz) ginger ale
a lemon twist, to garnish

Instructions
Pour the liqueur, wine and lemon juice into a flute. Top with the ginger ale, then garnish with a long lemon twist draped over the rim.

PIMM'S & ROSÉ

A British favourite, Pimm's No. 1 Cup is typically served with sparkling lemonade and enjoyed while watching tennis! The Pimm's & Rosé puts a twist on that classic drink, giving it a lovely kiss of blush wine while maintaining the traditional sparkle. This tall drink is very easy to mix up, and just as easily increased to fill a jug. The garnishes are key to the experience, so if you normally skip dressing up your drink, don't do that here. The cucumber adds a great hint of flavour, and borage is a herb with a similar taste (use the flowers, leaves or both). You can also add any combination of orange slices, strawberries or mint. Each garnish will contribute to the drink's flavour, so have fun customising it with any produce you find appealing as you shop.

Ingredients
30ml (1fl oz) Pimm's No. 1 Cup
90ml (3fl oz) sparkling rosé
3 cucumber slices
borage or mint leaves
strawberries and orange slices, to garnish

Instructions
Pour the Pimm's into a tall glass filled with ice. Top with the sparkling wine, then add cucumber slices, some borage or mint, berries and orange slices.

SPARKLING BORAGE COCKTAIL

Borage is not found in many cocktails, but it can be used to make some amazing drinks. The herb's flowers and young leaves taste surprisingly like cucumber. It takes on a dual role in the Sparkling Borage Cocktail, a floral martini that's sure to enhance your summer afternoons. For this recipe, you will need to make two ingredients with borage ahead of time – some borage ice cubes and a borage-flavoured syrup. If you don't grow your own borage, make sure you source it from somewhere that doesn't spray the plants with chemicals. Avoid older leaves as they lose their flavour; if you get pricked by a leaf, it's too old so don't use it.

Ingredients
a handful of borage flowers and young leaves
15ml (½fl oz) borage syrup
45ml (1½fl oz) gin
15ml (½fl oz) elderflower liqueur
a splash of lime juice
sparkling rosé, to top up

Instructions
Choose a few flowers that are in pristine condition to freeze into ice cubes: fill the tray halfway with distilled water and freeze, then add a flower to each cube, fill with water, then freeze again. It should take just over a day. The borage syrup is made by adding leaves and flowers to the Simple Syrup recipe on page 15. When you are ready to serve, add a few borage ice cubes to a chilled cocktail glass. Shake the borage syrup, gin, liqueur and lime juice with ice, then strain into the glass. Top up with sparkling wine.

ROSY RASPBERRY PRESS

A fresh take on the popular vodka press, this is a tall, refreshing and very fruity cocktail. It's a lot of fun to mix up and will give you a chance to learn a new bartending skill if you're up for the challenge. The vodka press is a rendition of the Presbyterian, a whisky highball that pairs soda water and lemon–lime soda. This recipe puts yet another twist (or three) on the recipe: muddling fresh raspberries and lime slices, switching to raspberry vodka, and skipping the second soda in lieu of sparkling rosé. The common way to mix a press is by 'rolling'. It's a technique bartenders like to use to show off, whereby you 'roll' a drink by pouring it back and forth between two glasses. Make sure your glasses are about the same size – pint glasses and cocktail shakers work well – and that they aren't filled to the rim. You might want to practise with iced water first. If you don't want to risk a spillage, just go ahead and stir the drink instead.

Ingredients
5 or 6 raspberries
2 lime slices
60ml (2fl oz) raspberry vodka
60ml (2fl oz) sparkling rosé
60ml (2fl oz) soda water

Instructions
In the bottom of a highball glass, muddle the raspberries and lime slices. Fill the glass partially with ice, add the vodka, wine and soda water, then roll the drink (or stir). If needed, add a couple more ice cubes before serving.

LIGHT PIÑA COLADA

Typically made with rum and cream of coconut, the piña colada is a perennial summertime cocktail. Why not try switching to a sweeter rosé wine and coconut water for a lighter version that is even more refreshing but has all the wonderful flavours you've come to love? The key to a really well-made piña colada is to give the drink a good shake before serving. The pineapple will froth up and, when it's strained, create a luscious foamy top that invites you in for each sip.

Ingredients
60ml (2fl oz) rosé
45ml (1 ½fl oz) coconut water
30ml (1fl oz) pineapple juice
a splash of lime juice
a pineapple wedge or lime slice, to garnish

Instructions
Pour the ingredients into a cocktail shaker filled with ice. Shake well then strain into a chilled coupe glass, garnishing with a pineapple wedge or lime slice.

ROSAQUIRI

Freshly made daiquiris beat any mix you can buy from a shop, and the recipe is so simple that it's a shame not to mix one up from scratch. The basic recipe requires rum, lime juice and Simple Syrup, with no secret ingredients. But as you would expect, we're going to add a spin to that recipe to create the fabulous Rosaquiri! Beyond adding rosé wine to the mix, this recipe uses a rosemary-flavoured syrup. It adds a lovely floral note to the cocktail, and you can use any leftover syrup to jazz up a simple glass of lemonade, or to sweeten a wine spritzer (see page 32).

Ingredients
15ml (½fl oz) rosemary syrup
60ml (2fl oz) rosé
45ml (1½fl oz) aged rum
15ml (½fl oz) lime juice
an extra sprig of rosemary and a lime wheel, to garnish

Instructions
Add a sprig or two of rosemary to the Simple Syrup recipe on page 15 and let it steep. Once cool, remove the rosemary from the syrup. Pour the rosemary syrup and all of the other ingredients into a cocktail shaker filled with ice and shake well. Strain into a chilled coupe glass and garnish with a small sprig of rosemary and a lime wheel.

ROSÉ SOUR

The Rosé Sour transforms the classic whisky sour into a beautiful drink to enjoy on a sunny day. It begins with a yellow Chartreuse rinse, which leaves your glass kissed with herbal sweetness. A smooth Irish whiskey and sweet rosé form the base, while the sour citrus is offset by a thyme-infused syrup. Egg white tops it all off with a luscious foam. Some people are reluctant to drink raw egg – and you can still enjoy this drink without it – but it's perfectly safe, as long as your egg is as fresh as possible. If you have concerns, try a quick freshness test: place the egg in a glass of water and if it sinks to the bottom, it's good!

Ingredients
15ml (½fl oz) thyme syrup
1 tspn yellow Chartreuse
white of 1 egg
45ml (1½fl oz) Irish whiskey
30ml (1fl oz) sweet rosé
30ml (1fl oz) lemon juice
2 dashes of orange bitters
lemon zest, to garnish

Instructions
Begin by infusing the Simple Syrup recipe on page 15 with 5 large sprigs of thyme. Rinse a cocktail glass with yellow Chartreuse by pouring in the liqueur, rolling it around to coat the inside of the glass, then getting rid of any excess. In a cocktail shaker without ice, dry-shake the egg white for about 10 seconds to break it up. Add ice and all the other ingredients. Shake vigorously for about 30 seconds, then strain into the prepared glass and garnish with a touch of lemon zest.

ROSÉ ROYALE

Pisco is a style of brandy produced in Peru and Chile,
which is famously used to make a pisco sour. That delicious
recipe is transformed here into the equally tasty Rosé Royale,
where it gets a kiss of sweet elderflower from a touch of
St-Germain liqueur. In true pisco sour fashion, an egg white
is added to lend a tempting foam. As with the Rosé Sour (see
page 78), the egg is perfectly fine to drink raw, as long as it
is very fresh. The base of the Rosé Royale is an enchanting
mix of pisco, elderflower, lime and rosé. The addition of
bitters on top then gives it an elegant touch that delights
you at first sip.

Ingredients
white of 1 egg
45ml (1½fl oz) pisco
15ml (½fl oz) St-Germain liqueur
15ml (½fl oz) lime juice
60ml (2fl oz) rosé
3 dashes of Angostura bitters

Instructions
Place the egg white in a cocktail shaker and dry-shake it for
about 10 seconds. Fill the shaker with ice, then add the pisco,
liqueur, lime juice and rosé. Shake vigorously for 30 seconds
and strain into a coupe glass. Finish with 3 dashes of bitters in
the foam.

GREEN & PINK LEMONADE

Green lemonade is great fun to make, and it's a recipe that is completely adaptable. It can be made with tequila, vodka and whisky, or alternatively it can be booze-free. It's also a perfect fit for rosé wines of any style. In the Green & Pink Lemonade, a sparkling rosé is a great choice, although you can achieve the same effect by pouring a still wine and adding a spritz of soda water. Fresh kiwis and equal parts limeade and lemonade are the common denominators in all of my green lemonade renditions. Kiwis are perfect against the sweetened citrus juices, and they're absolutely adorable as a garnish. Another lovely aspect of this recipe is that you can mix up the base and have a jug ready in the fridge, just waiting to be topped off with your choice of bubbly.

Ingredients
4 kiwi slices, skin removed
22ml (¾fl oz) Simple Syrup (see page 15)
45ml (1½fl oz) limeade
45ml (1½fl oz) lemonade
90ml (3fl oz) sparkling rosé
1 extra kiwi slice, to garnish

Instructions
Muddle the kiwi slices and Simple Syrup in the bottom of a tall glass. Fill with ice, then add the limeade and lemonade, finishing with the sparkling wine. Garnish with a slice of kiwi.

TEA FOR YOU & ME

(serves 2)

Afternoon tea for two can be made more interesting when you bring rum and rosé into the mix. This recipe is simple but unique, using a tea-infused rum as its base. White rum works best, but you can use any tea you like – green or black, or blends such as Earl Grey. Adding rosé and a lime–honey syrup, topped off with the drier profile of tonic, creates a well-balanced drink to enjoy with a friend.

Ingredients
90ml (3fl oz) tea-infused rum
240ml (8fl oz) water
120ml (4fl oz) honey
juice of 1 lime
120ml (4fl oz) rosé
60ml (2fl oz) tonic water
4 dashes of celery bitters (or orange bitters)
lime wedges, to garnish

Instructions
Place 2 teabags and 90ml (3fl oz) of white rum in a sealable container (the volume doesn't matter, so use a full bottle if you like) and let it sit at room temperature for a day to let the flavour develop fully. Bring the water to the boil in a small saucepan, then add the honey and lime juice. Stir, cover, reduce the heat and simmer for 5 minutes. Remove from the heat and leave, covered, to cool. It can be stored in a sealed container in the fridge for about one week. For the cocktail, fill two tall glasses with ice. Pour the ingredients in order equally between the two glasses. Stir well and garnish with the lime wedges.

SUMMER ROMANCE

Creamy and fruity, you're sure to fall in love with the Summer Romance. This sweet tequila blend makes a delightful after-dinner drink on a relaxed summer evening. Tequila is classified according to how long it is left to age. Reposado tequila is a lightly aged style that spends around two to nine months in oak barrels, giving the agave-based spirit a pleasant oak flavour that works wonderfully when mixed into a cocktail. Here it is blended with the spiced honey taste of Benedictine liqueur and sweet raspberries. The coconut lends a luscious creaminess, while the sparkling rosé ensures a lively finish.

Ingredients
6 raspberries
45ml (1½fl oz) reposado tequila
15ml (½fl oz) Benedictine
15ml (½fl oz) cream of coconut
60ml (2fl oz) sparkling rosé
extra raspberries, to garnish

Instructions
Muddle the raspberries in the bottom of an old-fashioned glass. Add ice, then pour the remaining ingredients in order. Stir well and garnish with a few extra raspberries.

LA ROSA PALOMA

Rosé and strawberries are a fun way to dress up the popular tequila-based cocktail, the paloma. As with the original recipe, this appealing variation features the refreshing taste of grapefruit, which comes into play via a flavoured sparkling water, making it a great choice for summer, and particularly enjoyable for an afternoon picnic. La Rosa Paloma is a quick drink to mix up, too. While you might be tempted to skip the rosemary garnish, give it a try if you have the herb around. A small sprig will slowly infuse its flavour into your drink as it sits on top, providing a graceful finishing touch. You can also add a little rosemary into the muddle for a stronger taste.

Ingredients
15ml (½fl oz) lime juice
2 strawberries, sliced
45ml (1½fl oz) blanco tequila
60ml (2fl oz) rosé
90ml (3fl oz) grapefruit-flavoured sparkling water
1 grapefruit slice and a sprig of rosemary, to garnish

Instructions
In the bottom of a highball glass, muddle the lime juice and sliced strawberries. Fill the glass with ice, add the tequila and wine, then top it off with the sparkling water. Finish with a grapefruit slice and rosemary sprig, to garnish.

PINK NEGRONI

The Negroni is a fabulous aperitif that can be enjoyed before any meal. The original gin-and-Campari recipe has been remade many times since its creation in the 1920s. One of the most popular variations gives it a bubbly twist, and in the Pink Negroni, we're going with a lovely French rosé Champagne. Campari is the key to any negroni. This Italian aperitif has a bitter flavour that takes some getting used to, but it pairs perfectly with gin, and this recipe offers a particularly gentle introduction to the Campari taste, softening it with port (tawny or ruby ports are best) and the sweet black-raspberry addition of Chambord. It's an elegant cocktail worthy of a special dinner, no matter what's on the menu.

Ingredients
30ml (1fl oz) gin
15ml (½fl oz) Campari
15ml (½fl oz) port
7.5ml (¼fl oz) Chambord
rosé Champagne, to top up

Instructions
Pour the gin, Campari, port and Chambord into a flute. Top up with rosé Champagne and let the bubbles do the mixing for you.

ROSÉ PARADE

The Rosé Parade is definitely a fun rosé martini – the emphasis here is on the presentation, which makes the tropical fruit flavour even more enjoyable. The fun begins with rosé ice cubes, which are then adorned with three balls of fresh papaya. The drink itself is a combination of guava nectar and sparkling rosé, and there's no mixing involved – the bubbles take care of that for you. The rosé cubes mean that you can enjoy this one as slowly as you like, too; you won't need to worry about ending up with a watered-down drink, no matter how warm the weather is.

Ingredients
5 rosé ice cubes
3 papaya balls
30ml (1fl oz) guava nectar
90ml (3fl oz) sparkling rosé

Instructions
Make the rosé ice cubes by filling an ice cube tray with still rosé wine. Add fruits or herbs such as raspberries or rosemary to the cubes if you like. Let them freeze overnight and remove them from the freezer just before making the cocktail. Use a melon baller to scoop out balls of papaya. (These can also be frozen ahead of time, if you prefer – simply spread them out in a single layer to keep them separate.) Place 5 rosé cubes and 3 papaya balls in a cocktail glass. Top with the guava nectar and finish with the sparkling rosé.

BIRTHDAY CAKE MIMOSA

This adorable-looking mimosa is the ultimate way to celebrate someone's birthday! The drink is pretty delicious, too, recreating the yummy flavours of a sweet birthday cake in a flute. The base of this cocktail is a mix of sweet cake-flavoured vodka (whipped-cream vodka also works well) and coconut water. A sparkling rosé then gives it the mimosa touch. But it's the rim of this cocktail, with its vanilla frosting and colourful sprinkles, that truly transforms it into a drink to toast someone's special day.

Ingredients
vanilla frosting (buttercream)
coloured sprinkles
45ml (1 ½fl oz) cake-flavoured vodka
15ml (½fl oz) coconut water
sparkling rosé, to top up

Instructions
Dip the rim of a flute into a dish of vanilla frosting, rolling it around to get a good coating. Then dip the rim into a second small dish filled with coloured sprinkles. Pour the cake-flavoured vodka and coconut water into the prepared glass, then top up with your sparkling rosé.

BLUSHING FIZZ

The Blushing Fizz features lavender–vanilla syrup, an ingredient that's a personal favourite and useful for creating the loveliest drinks. Here, that soft flavour is paired with the spicy sweetness of ginger liqueur (Domaine de Canton is an excellent choice). Sparkling rosé then invigorates the blend to create a highly enjoyable drink. This recipe also features another fun ingredient – lavender ice cubes, which can be made by adding lavender flowers to a filled ice cube tray before freezing. You can also make the cubes a little sweeter by adding some of the lavender–vanilla syrup.

Ingredients
30ml (1fl oz) lavender–vanilla syrup
15ml (½fl oz) lemon juice
45ml (1½fl oz) ginger liqueur
lavender ice cubes
sparkling rosé, to top up
a lemon twist or edible flowers, to garnish

Instructions
Begin by creating the syrup by adding 7g (¼oz) of lavender buds and a vanilla pod to the Simple Syrup recipe on page 15. In a cocktail shaker filled with ice, combine the syrup, lemon juice and liqueur. Shake well then strain into a tall glass filled with lavender ice cubes. Top up with rosé then garnish with a lemon twist; or if you're in the mood to get fancy, decorate this cocktail with edible flowers – roses, nasturtiums, borage and hibiscus are all fun options. Just ensure that the plants have not been sprayed with pesticides or other chemicals – even if you're not going to eat the garnish (a social faux pas, but who's looking!).

ROSÉ POPTAIL

Poptails are the adult answer to frozen ice lollies, and you can add all sorts of alcohol, juice and fruits. The Rosé Poptail is a great introduction and, because wine is the only alcohol involved, you'll have no problems getting it to freeze. Lolly moulds are easy to find and usually make four to six lollies at a time. Because the sizes vary, this recipe is written in parts rather than exact measurements. Simply figure out the total volume needed and divide it between the two liquids. (Or make a little more than you need and enjoy any leftovers while you wait for the lollies to freeze!) Don't forget to buy the sticks if your mould doesn't include them.

Ingredients
½ part ruby red grapefruit juice
1 part rosé
raspberries
blackberries

Instructions
Combine the grapefruit juice and wine in a jug and stir well. Fill each mould three-quarters of the way up. Add a few berries to each mould; when you do this will depend on where you want them placed. For berries at the top of the lolly, add them right away because they will sink in the mould. If you want berries in the middle and closer to the stick, add them after the mixture has become become slushy. You can also add a berry or two later in the freezing process for even distribution. Once all the berries are in place, top up the moulds with your wine-juice mix. A fun way to serve these is to chill a Mason jar, then fill it halfway with a chilled sparkling wine. Turn a Rosé Poptail upside down and stick it in the glass. You get an iced wine to drink and an edible treat at the same time!

SAGE GIMLET

Simple, sophisticated and offering a lovely mix of flavours, the Sage Gimlet puts a wine-and-herb twist on a cocktail that has long been a favourite. Typically, a gimlet is nothing more than gin and lime cordial, and this recipe keeps it fairly simple. The key ingredient here is the sage–lime syrup; adding this to a full-flavoured gin, then finishing it off with a soft rosé creates a cocktail that is perfect for an afternoon in the garden.

Ingredients
15ml (½fl oz) sage–lime syrup
45ml (1½fl oz) rosé
45ml (1½fl oz) gin
an extra sage leaf, to garnish

Instructions
Add a few sage leaves and the juice of 1 lime to the Simple Syrup recipe on page 15, then remove the leaves after it cools. In a cocktail shaker filled with ice, combine all the ingredients then shake well. Strain into a chilled cocktail glass and garnish with a single sage leaf floating on top.

ROSÉ SUNRISE

The tequila sunrise is a showy cocktail filled with fruit flavours, which has led to its immense popularity over the years. It's also the perfect recipe for a twist, and the Rosé Sunrise definitely throws a few in. This drink allows Grand Marnier to take over the orange element, while a grapefruit-infused tequila enhances the citrus aspect. Instead of orange juice, it's filled with brut (dry) rosé, giving it a lovely balance and softer profile. The grenadine not only produces the signature sunrise effect, but also adds a sweet pomegranate fruitiness that brings it all together. The grapefruit tequila is incredibly easy to make, though you'll need to plan ahead.

Ingredients
45ml (1½fl oz) grapefruit-infused tequila
30ml (1fl oz) Grand Marnier
dry rosé, to top up
7.5ml (¼fl oz) grenadine
½ grapefruit slice and a cherry, to garnish

Instructions
To make the grapefruit tequila, remove the peel from a whole grapefruit, then slice the fruit and place it in an infusion jar with 720ml (24fl oz) of tequila. Give it a good shake, and let the flavour develop for 3 to 5 days, shaking it once daily. Strain out the grapefruit, bottle the tequila, and you're ready to make a sunrise! You will need 45ml (1½fl oz) of the infusion for this recipe. Combine the tequila and Grand Marnier in a hurricane glass (or other tall glass) filled with ice. Top up with rosé. Slowly pour the grenadine around the inside of the glass. It will sink and gradually rise to mix with the other ingredients. Garnish with half a grapefruit slice and a cherry.

SWEET HONEY ROSÉ

There's a very simple cocktail called the bee's knees that became a hit during Prohibition in America. It was used as a way to doctor up the less-than-desirable 'bathtub' gin of the time by adding honey syrup and lemon juice. The Sweet Honey Rosé reimagines this old-time favourite to create an equally fascinating drink that mixes up in minutes. In this recipe, gin is replaced with whisky – a smooth blend like Irish whiskey is a fantastic choice – and retains the honey syrup and lemon juice. The final ingredient is, of course, rosé. Almost any wine will do and it's best to experiment with a few to find one that matches your taste. Some people may like a sweeter rosé, such as a white zinfandel, while others may prefer a wine with a drier profile.

Ingredients
15ml (½fl oz) honey
15ml (½fl oz) water
45ml (1½fl oz) whisky
a splash of lemon juice
45ml (1½fl oz) rosé

Instructions
There are no secrets to making honey syrup: combine equal parts honey and water and stir until you get a uniform consistency. It's a simple trick that thins out the honey just enough to make it easier to mix in cold drinks. Combine all the ingredients in a cocktail shaker filled with ice. Shake well and strain into a chilled cocktail glass.

LYCHEE GINGER MARTINI

A lychee tastes like a strawberry (hence the nickname 'alligator strawberry') and it pairs wonderfully with many flavours, from citrus to cranberry, but it's also a surprising companion for ginger. It is becoming easier to find lychee-flavoured liqueurs and syrups on the market, but the other option is to make one of these yourself, using fresh or canned fruits (which have had the inedible hulls removed). The ginger vodka can also be a homemade project because it's not the most common flavour among vodka brands. If you don't want to go to that extent, you can use unflavoured vodka and enjoy a rosé lychee martini.

Ingredients
45ml (1½fl oz) lychee liqueur or syrup
45ml (1½fl oz) ginger vodka
45ml (1½fl oz) rosé
a lychee or lemon twist, to garnish

Instructions
Pour the ingredients into a cocktail shaker filled with ice and shake well. Strain into a chilled cocktail glass, then garnish with a lychee or lemon twist.

If making your own lychee syrup, use 85g (3oz) lychees in the Simple Syrup recipe on page 15. To make a lychee liqueur, add 120ml (4fl oz) of lychee syrup to 375ml (12fl oz) of vodka, adding more to taste, if desired. For a homemade ginger vodka, add 50g (1¾oz) of ginger slices to 750ml (25fl oz) vodka in a jar and leave for up to 7 days. Shake daily and strain out the ginger once it reaches your desired flavour.

SNOW ROSE

The Snow Rose is one of the most beautiful drinks you'll have the pleasure of sipping. Whenever you shake a cocktail with pineapple juice, a luscious foam forms on top of the drink after straining. This cocktail takes full advantage of that because you'll drizzle pink rose water over the foam and swirl it gently to create the effect of rose petals on a bed of snow. Make sure your rose water is the food-safe variety, not a product made for cosmetic use. Some rose water is pink while others are clear. If you can only find the clear variety, stir in a small amount of rosé to give it a hint of colour.

Ingredients
30ml (1fl oz) aged rum
30ml (1fl oz) rosé
30ml (1fl oz) pineapple juice
a splash of Simple Syrup (see page 15)
a drizzle of rose water

Instructions
Pour the rum, wine, juice and syrup into a cocktail shaker filled with ice. Shake vigorously and strain into a chilled cocktail glass. Drizzle the rose water on top of the foam and give it a quick swirl with a spoon or a small stick.

Tip: If you have pesticide-free rose plants, you can harvest the petals to make your own rose water. Rinse the petals from two roses, then combine them in a small saucepan with 480ml (16fl oz) of distilled water and a teaspoon of vodka. Simmer, covered, for about 30 minutes, or until the petals become pale. Remove from the heat, strain and bottle. This will keep in the fridge for about 2 weeks (the vodka acts as a preservative).

WILD IRISH ROSÉ

Irish whiskey and rosé are a very nice duo and they find perfect harmony in the lovely Wild Irish Rosé, where they're sweetened with a combination of pomegranate and cherry liqueurs. Using a sparkling wine transforms this into an effervescent beverage that's fantastic anytime you feel the desire for a unique whisky highball. Cherry Heering is called for specifically because it's one of the best cherry-flavoured liqueurs available. It's sweet, with a deep red colour, but it lacks that medicinal taste that is so common in spirits of this flavour, which is why it's a great choice for cocktails. The next best option is maraschino liqueur. It's a little drier, so it's a good option if you prefer drinks that are less sweet.

Ingredients

30ml (1fl oz) Irish whiskey
15ml (½fl oz) pomegranate liqueur
15ml (½fl oz) Cherry Heering
90ml (3fl oz) sparkling rosé, to top up
a dash of orange bitters
a cherry, to garnish

Instructions

Combine the whiskey and liqueurs in a collins glass filled with ice. Stir for 30 seconds, then top up with sparkling rosé. Add a dash of orange bitters and garnish with a cherry.

MIDNIGHT ROSÉ FLOAT

An ice cream float combines a soft drink with vanilla ice cream. Skip the soft drink and make yourself a delicious ice cream treat with rosé instead! The Midnight Rosé Float is a fun recipe that throws all pretentions associated with wine out of the window. It's definitely one of the most indulgent wine drinks you can mix up, but it also has a touch of class. For this recipe, you'll use a mix of brandy, Grand Marnier and rosé as the liquid portion of the ice cream float. The hint of orange from the brandy-based liqueur adds a soft, sweet fruitiness that is intriguing against the other ingredients. You could even add another dimension by choosing an apricot or cherry brandy, if you like.

Ingredients
1 scoop vanilla ice cream
45ml (1½fl oz) brandy
22ml (¾fl oz) Grand Marnier
60ml (2fl oz) rosé
chocolate syrup and a raspberry, to garnish

Instructions
Place a scoop of ice cream in the bottom of a parfait glass and put it in the freezer while you mix the rest of the drink. In a cocktail shaker filled with ice, combine the brandy, Grand Marnier and wine and shake well. Strain over the ice cream, then drizzle with chocolate syrup and garnish with a raspberry.

ROSÉ COLLINS

The collins is a classic mixed-drink formula of a base spirit, combined with a sweetener, a sour element and soda water. Any distilled spirit is up for grabs: whisky and gin are the most popular, although vodka, rum and tequila are also good choices. In the Rosé Collins, whisky – specifically bourbon – is the spirit of choice, and the soda water is replaced with a sparkling rosé. The fun elements of this collins are the sweet and sour ingredients. It opts for honey syrup (a mix of equal parts honey and water) along with a muddle of cucumber slices and a lemon wedge. These add a fresh-produce spin on the drink that turns it into an absolute delight for the warmer seasons.

Ingredients
15ml (½fl oz) honey
15ml (½fl oz) water
3 cucumber slices
a lemon wedge
45ml (1½fl oz) bourbon
sparkling rosé, to top up
extra cucumber and lemon slices, to garnish

Instructions
Combine the honey and water and stir until you get a uniform consistency. In a highball glass, muddle the syrup, cucumber slices and lemon wedge. Fill the glass with ice, add the whisky, stir thoroughly, and top up with rosé. Garnish with a slice each of cucumber and lemon.

VIOLETS & ROSES

Crème de violette is an often overlooked liqueur, but it's a perfect ingredient for rosé cocktails. This violet-flavoured, eye-catching purple liqueur offers a beautiful floral fragrance and taste. It's the star of the aviation cocktail, a delightful gin martini, and the Violets & Roses is a modern adaptation of that classic, simply replacing the gin with rosé. In keeping with its roots, you'll likely find it at its best when made with a high-end Provençal rosé. The drier profile mimics that of gin, and this cocktail really deserves the best wine you feel comfortable pouring. When the violets and wine are accented with the cherry of a dry maraschino liqueur and fresh lemon juice, you will have an exquisite cocktail that is guaranteed to impress anyone.

Ingredients
60ml (2fl oz) rosé
15ml (½fl oz) maraschino liqueur
22ml (¾fl oz) crème de violette
15ml (½fl oz) lemon juice
a lemon twist, to garnish

Instructions
Combine all of the ingredients in a cocktail shaker filled with ice. Shake well and strain into a chilled cocktail glass, garnishing with a lemon twist.

ROSEMARY & BASIL FIZZ

Finding drinks that you can make with ingredients from your own garden always makes the harvest that much more satisfying, and this one is the perfect drink to sit back with as you relax and survey the fruits of your labour. This is also a great recipe for anyone who enjoys homemade mixers. Sure, you may be able to find a cucumber vodka in the shops (and Hendrick's Gin is a good substitute), but it's a very easy infusion to make yourself if you plan ahead.

Ingredients
45ml (1½fl oz) cucumber vodka
15ml (½fl oz) rosemary–basil syrup
15ml (½fl oz) lime juice
90ml (3fl oz) sparkling rosé
a sprig of rosemary, to garnish

Instructions
If you want to make your own cucumber vodka, add one cucumber – skin removed and sliced into small pieces – to 750ml (25fl oz) of vodka. Shake it daily and taste it after 3 days, then every day thereafter until it reaches your desired flavour (it can take up to 2 weeks). Strain out the cucumber and bottle the vodka.

For the rosemary–basil syrup, add 1 sprig of rosemary and 20g (¾oz) of basil leaves to the Simple Syrup recipe on page 15.

Pour the ingredients in order into an ice-filled Mason jar (or another tall glass), finishing up with the wine. Stir well and garnish with a sprig of rosemary.

JASMINE TEA TINI

A tea-flavoured martini is a great choice as an afternoon drink, and jasmine tea is a wonderful, fragrant option. It's particularly nice when paired with rosé in a simple and elegant vodka martini recipe. The Jasmine Tea Tini is easy to prepare and you can adjust each of the elements to suit your personal taste. Start by pouring equal parts of the vodka and rosé, then increase either while reducing the quantity of tea, if you like. Then add more of either the Simple Syrup or lemon juice as you see fit. This is also a lovely recipe to mix up by the jug and serve at a small gathering: keep everything in proportion and increase the pour of each ingredient according to the number of servings you need. You can stir it with ice in the jug, then pour it into cocktail glasses to serve.

Ingredients
30ml (1fl oz) vodka
30ml (1fl oz) rosé
60ml (2fl oz) jasmine tea, chilled
a splash of Simple Syrup (see page 15)
a splash of lemon juice
a jasmine flower or lemon twist, to garnish

Instructions
In a cocktail shaker filled with ice, combine the ingredients. Shake well and strain into a chilled cocktail glass. If available, garnish with a jasmine flower; otherwise use a long lemon twist.

POINSETTIA SANGRIA

(serves 5)

Who says sangria should be reserved for summer? This wine punch is just as appropriate for winter celebrations as it is for any other time of year, especially if you have the right recipe. The Poinsettia Sangria plays up the best flavours of the Christmas season, and makes a wonderful addition to any holiday soirée. It features pomegranates and cranberries, both of which come into their prime as the weather begins to cool down, while the cinnamon syrup adds a warming touch that makes this drink a real winter delight.

Ingredients

60ml (2fl oz) cinnamon syrup
2 pomegranates
750ml (25fl oz) rosé
240ml (8fl oz) rum
100g (3½oz) cranberries
2 oranges, sliced
extra cranberries or pomegranate arils (seeds), to garnish

Instructions

Infuse the Simple Syrup recipe on page 15 with a stick of cinnamon. Remove the arils from the pomegranates and reserve a few for the garnish. Smash the rest of the arils in a bowl, then strain them so you are left with a fresh juice. Combine the juice with the remaining ingredients in a jug, stir well and refrigerate overnight to allow the flavours to marry. Serve in tumblers or punch cups and garnish with cranberries or pomegranate arils.

PASSIONFRUIT SANGRIA

(serves 12)

There's a lot going on in this very fruity sangria! It's a fun blend of tropical fruit flavours, including passionfruit, pineapple and kiwi, so it's ideal for summer barbecues and pool parties. The recipe makes a lot of punch, too, so you can quench the thirst of all your guests with a single batch. As with any sangria, this one's all about the fresh fruit. Fresh lemon, orange and kiwi are included, but if you spot passionfruit and pineapples at the supermarket, you can add some chunks of those as well. The Passionfruit Sangria is best with a sweeter rosé; white zinfandel is an excellent choice.

Ingredients
750ml (25fl oz) sweet rosé
240ml (8fl oz) brandy
480ml (16fl oz) passionfruit juice
480ml (16fl oz) pineapple juice
1 lemon, sliced
1 orange, sliced
2 kiwis, sliced
480ml (16fl oz) ginger ale

Instructions
Combine all of the ingredients except the ginger ale in a large bowl, stir well and refrigerate overnight so the flavours blend and develop fully. When it's time to serve, add the ginger ale and ladle into punch cups. Kiwi slices make a great garnish, but they're not necessary if you ladle fruit into the glasses.

WHITE PEACH SANGRIA

(serves 10)

Rosé is a perfect wine for a sangria featuring the sweet taste of white peaches. This punch is perfect for summer, when these delectable fruits make their annual appearance in shops everywhere. The recipe will provide enough for a small party, and all of your guests will enjoy this refreshing, light twist on the classic sangria. This sangria is not all about the peach, either! It also includes the tropical taste of a mango-flavoured rum. Adding lemons and limes to the mix creates a bright, fruity drink that is unforgettable.

Ingredients

750ml (25fl oz) rosé
360ml (12fl oz) mango-flavoured rum
360ml (12fl oz) peach liqueur
4 white peaches, sliced
2 limes, sliced
2 lemons, sliced
600ml (20fl oz) soda water
extra peach slices, to garnish

Instructions

In a large jug or bowl, combine the wine, rum, liqueur and all the sliced fruit. Refrigerate overnight to allow the flavours to marry. Before serving, add the soda water. Pour into glasses over ice (if you like) and garnish with slices of white peach.

If you want to create your own mango-infused rum, chop a whole mango into small cubes and infuse it in your chosen quantity of rum for at least a week before removing the fruit.

GREEN GRAPE SANGRIA

(serves 8)

Grapes make a fantastic sangria year-round and they're another fabulous pairing for rosé wine. In the Green Grape Sangria, the grapes actually serve as a substitute for ice, offering all of the chill with none of the dilution, and a little extra flavour. The base of this sangria is a still rosé, then a sparkling version is added at the end to give it a nice fizz. White grape juice is much lighter and less sweet than the regular purple juice, so it's a much better fit for this recipe. If you'd like, use freshly pressed green grape juice instead.

Ingredients
600g (21oz) green grapes
2 lemons, sliced
750ml (25fl oz) still rosé
480ml (16fl oz) white grape juice
60ml (2fl oz) agave nectar
375ml (13fl oz) sparkling rosé

Instructions
Flash-freeze half of the grapes in a single layer in the freezer. Once frozen, they can be transferred to a bowl or bag for easy storage. In a glass, muddle the remaining grapes with the lemon slices, mashing them until all the juice is extracted. Strain out the lemon pieces and grape skins, leaving a clean juice behind. In a large jug, combine the grape–lemon juice with the still wine, white grape juice and agave nectar. Stir thoroughly. Distribute the frozen grapes between 8 glasses, fill each three-quarters full with the sangria mix, then top with the sparkling rosé.

CARAMEL APPLE SANGRIA

(serves 10)

This punch provides a delicious way to celebrate autumn. It uses the same caramel syrup you use to flavour your coffee, and by combining it with apple cider and freshly harvested apples, the sangria takes on a very seasonal flair. If you prefer, switch from plain vodka to a caramel-flavoured vodka and use plain Simple Syrup (see page 15) to sweeten the punch instead. Since you'll likely make this in apple season, try to get your hands on some freshly pressed cider. And try to find the most flavoursome sparkling rosé you can. Although it plays a supporting role (bubbles) in this recipe, a lighter-profiled wine can easily get lost among all the other flavours.

Ingredients

240ml (8fl oz) vodka
60ml (2fl oz) caramel syrup
720ml (24fl oz) apple cider
3 red apples, cored and sliced
750ml (25fl oz) sparkling rosé
extra apple slices, to garnish

Instructions

In a jug, combine the vodka, syrup and cider and stir. Add the apple slices and refrigerate overnight. Just before serving, add the sparkling wine. Serve in stemmed wine glasses (over ice if you prefer) and garnish with apple slices.

Tip: Apple slices will quickly turn brown due to oxidation, so to keep your garnish looking beautiful, dip your slices into a little lemon juice, then shake off the excess.

RASPBERRY LEMONADE SANGRIA

(serves 8)

The peak of summer is an ideal time to mix up a Raspberry Lemonade Sangria. If you have a raspberry bush in the garden, it's even better and will make quick use of your harvest. Your guests will be delighted with the sweet, refreshing taste of this sangria, and you will be thrilled with how easy it is to make. The best advice is to keep it as fresh as possible – after all, summer is about enjoying the freshest ingredients – so take the time to make the lemonade and Simple Syrup from scratch. For the wine, any rosé will do, although this is the perfect recipe for a white zinfandel.

Ingredients

360ml (12fl oz) lemonade
750ml (25fl oz) rosé
250g (9oz) fresh raspberries
2 lemons, sliced
60ml (2fl oz) Simple Syrup (see page 15)
360ml (12fl oz) ginger ale
extra lemon slices and raspberries, to garnish

Instructions

To make fresh lemonade, stir together 1 part each of fresh lemon juice and Simple Syrup with 2 parts distilled water. Add more of any ingredient to suit your taste. Mix this lemonade together with the rosé, raspberries, lemon slices and Simple Syrup in a large jug. Refrigerate overnight. Just before serving, add the ginger ale. Serve over ice, garnishing each glass with a slice of lemon and a few raspberries.

ROSÉ BERRY BLISS

(serves 10)

When you serve the Rosé Berry Bliss at a party, it's bound to brighten everyone's mood. This brilliant wine and lemonade punch is unbelievably simple and has a tasty fruit flavour that all your guests will love. And if you need to make a larger batch, the quantities are easy to double or triple. The beauty of this particular recipe is that the ingredients are easy to find. While fresh blueberries are preferable, frozen berries will do just fine out of season. Most supermarkets now stock pink lemonade, and from there, all you need is a bottle of rosé and some citrus-flavoured soda water.

Ingredients

750ml (25fl oz) rosé
100g (3½oz) blueberries
960ml (32fl oz) pink lemonade
1 litre (34fl oz) lemon–lime soda water
extra blueberries, to garnish

Instructions

In a jug, combine the rosé, blueberries and lemonade and stir well. Set aside in the fridge for at least one hour to allow the flavours to marry. Add the soda water just before serving. Serve in flutes and garnish with blueberries.

ROSÉ ERDBEERBOWLE

(serves 8)

Erdbeerbowle means 'strawberry punch' in German and is
a very popular summer party drink. This is possibly the most
strawberry of all strawberry punches. It requires both still
and sparkling wines, and making it is a bit of a process,
so be sure to plan ahead. You'll need to macerate the
strawberries in sugar and lemon juice for a couple of hours,
then marinate them in the still rosé for a couple more. It is
worth it, though, and your guests will appreciate your efforts!

Ingredients
900g (30oz) strawberries, washed, hulled and sliced
100g (3½oz) white granulated sugar
zest and juice of 2 lemons
750ml (25fl oz) still rosé
750ml (25fl oz) sparkling rosé
fresh mint leaves or lemon balm, to garnish

Instructions
Place the strawberries in a bowl and cover with the sugar.
Add the lemon zest and juice to the strawberries, cover and
refrigerate for 2 hours. Separate the strawberries from the juice
and set the juice aside. Pour the still rosé over the strawberries
and marinate for 1 to 2 hours in the fridge. When ready to
serve, transfer the strawberry–wine mixture to a punch bowl
along with the strawberry juice, then add the sparkling wine.
Ladle the punch into glasses, including plenty of strawberries in
each. Garnish with mint or lemon balm and offer small forks or
cocktail sticks so guests can skewer the berries as they drink.

CANTALOUPE PUNCH

(serves 4)

When cantaloupe melons are in season, this easy punch is a delightful addition to a small party. It's ideal for summer and would be a nice complement to a casual brunch featuring fresh fruits and delicate pastries. It's also a fun option at a barbecue because it's such a good pairing for any grilled meat or kebabs. The Cantaloupe Punch focuses on fresh summer fruits, pairing the melon with sweet peaches. There's even a little gin to give it a nice botanical twist; any gin will do, even the lightly flavoured and rosier ones. Since the fruits are the only sweet elements in this recipe, you'll find that it's best with a sweet rosé.

Ingredients
½ cantaloupe melon, peeled and cubed
2 peaches, sliced
120ml (4fl oz) gin
750ml (25fl oz) rosé

Instructions
Combine all the ingredients in a jug, stir well, then refrigerate overnight to allow the flavours to marry. Serve in tall glasses, making sure to include pieces of fruit in each.

ROSÉ BOWL

(serves 4)

One of the most entertaining things you can do in a cocktail bar is to sit around a table with a group of friends slurping a boozy punch out of a fishbowl. It's a great time for all, and you can recreate that experience at home with the Rosé Bowl. This recipe features gin, and it's an excellent opportunity to use some of the lighter gins on the market – or any that take a unique approach to the juniper-forward standard. This punch is super-rosy and invigorating with its combination of rosé and grapefruit juice. Be sure to go all out on the fruits you mix into the ice! There are no rules, but the more fruit you add, the better and more exotic it will be.

Ingredients
120ml (4fl oz) gin
300ml (10fl oz) rosé
60ml (2fl oz) orange liqueur
240ml (8fl oz) ruby red grapefruit juice
grapefruit slices
seasonal berries

Instructions
Fill a fishbowl about halfway with ice and pour in all of the ingredients. Add the fruits, then stir well to mix everything together. Place the bowl in the middle of the table and use four long straws to enjoy it with your friends.

Tip: Fishbowl cocktail glasses are available to buy, and typically hold over a litre (34fl oz) – more than enough for this recipe, including the ice and fruit. You can also use an actual fishbowl, but clean it very, very well if it's had previous inhabitants!

CREDITS

Colleen Graham would like to thank:
My husband, Shannon, for his patience and support as well as his willingness to test any drink I'm mixing up.

My gratitude also goes out to all my colleagues and contacts in the writing, bar, distilling and wine industries who have offered information and inspiration over the years, contributing to the drink encyclopaedia that fills my mind.

For further reading about wine, I highly recommend *The Wine Bible* by Karen MacNeil, and Kevin Zraley's *Windows on the World Complete Wine Course*. Both will answer many questions about the complex world of wine, even those you didn't know to ask.

Finally, if you're now inspired to dive into unique flavour pairings in your drinks, *The Flavor Bible* by Karen Page and Andrew Dornenburg is an absolutely essential reference.

Ruby Taylor would like to thank:
For all the love, support (and drinks) always –
Katie Price, Nancy Edmondson, Billie Alder,
Ella Antebi, Roxanne Simmonds, Pema Seely,
Ellie Yates, Anita Kershaw.